Pearls *of* Wisdom *from* Hinduism

Best Wishes
Nick Sutton

Pearls *of* Wisdom *from* Hinduism

Hanuman Dass
Nicholas Sutton

JAICO PUBLISHING HOUSE
Ahmedabad Bangalore Bhopal Bhubaneswar Chennai
Delhi Hyderabad Kolkata Lucknow Mumbai

Published by Jaico Publishing House
A-2 Jash Chambers, 7-A Sir Phirozshah Mehta Road
Fort, Mumbai - 400 001
jaicopub@jaicobooks.com
www.jaicobooks.com

PEARLS OF WISDOM FROM HINDUISM
ISBN 978-81-8495-834-8

First Jaico Impression: 2017

Page design and layout: Jojy Philip, Delhi

Printed by
Thomson Press (India) Limited
B-315, Okhla Industrial Area, Phase-1
New Delhi - 110 020

Lead us from untruth to truth,
Lead us from darkness to light,
Lead us from death to immortality,
OM shanti, shanti, shanti.

CONTENTS

Introduction xi

1. The Foundation of Hinduism 2
2. Core Principles 5
3. The Superior Understanding 8
4. Qualities of Good People 11
5. Love Everybody 14
6. Compassion 17
7. Non-Harming 20
8. Kindness to All 23
9. Tuladhara's Rule of Life 26
10. The Mark of Dharma 29
11. Cruelty 32
12. Avoiding Meat 35
13. The Karma of Eating 38
14. Noble Aspirations 41
15. True Happiness 44
16. Truth 47
17. Bad Karma 50
18. Greed 53
19. The Right Versus the Pleasurable 56
20. A Message for Students 59

21. The Mother 63
22. The Sky and the Earth 66
23. Longing and Separation 69
24. O Goddess 73
25. Caste: Birth or Qualities? 76
26. Reverence for Cows 79
27. Be Like Trees 82
28. Waters! 86
29. Who Really Knows? 89
30. Act as You See Fit 92
31. Dedication to God 95
32. Om! 98
33. Reincarnation 101
34. Polish the Mirror 104
35. The End of Suffering 107
36. Age After Age 110
37. Do You Know Brahman? 113
38. Essence Seekers 116
39. Like Rivers to the Sea 119
40. Completeness 123
41. It's All in the Heart 126
42. Brahman Offering to Brahman 129
43. Brahman 132
44. Self-Realization 135
45. I am Brahman 138
46. Awakened Knowing 141
47. Like a Spider's Web 144
48. Desire 147
49. God in All Beings 150

50. Birds on a Tree 153
51. Devotion and Knowledge 156
52. The Nature of God 159
53. The Eternal Element 162
54. One Truth, Many Names 165
55. One Fire, Many Flames 168
56. Shiva and Vishnu 171
57. I am the Atman 174
58. Like Jewels on a Thread 177
59. The Origin 180
60. Non-Coveting 183
61. Only Love 186
62. Whom Krishna Loves 189
63. The Love of the Gopis 192
64. The Mood of Devotion 195
65. Controlling the Mind 198
66. Yoga and Action 201
67. What is Yoga? 204
68. Yoga Posture 207
69. Engaged in Yoga 210
70. Kundalini 213
71. Destiny Versus Endeavour 216
72. Following the Sanatana Dharma 219

INTRODUCTION

I consider this book a journey, a sacred pilgrimage through Hinduism, through the ancient tradition that is Sanatana Dharma. This collection of seventy-two verses has been carefully chosen from a vast corpus of religious literature, in the hope of providing a foundation for understanding the essence of Hinduism. These are voices from a period of great antiquity, but are just as relevant today as they were when they were spoken thousands of years ago. Being the oldest of the world's major religious traditions and the faith of over a billion people, the wisdom of Hindu doctrines and religious practices have enriched countless lives for thousands of years. These ancient traditions provide us with precious maps to higher states of consciousness, guide us to living virtuous lives, and provide us with a profoundly deep sense of fulfilment. They teach us a tangible path to living a happy life, and ultimately help us to create a better, safer world.

I believe that internalizing these high-minded ideals into one's life can have a transformative effect and provide a spark of light in an all too dark world. These verses are like precious tools that can help us not only cope with suffering, but also shift our focus from the pervading materialistic worldview to one based on overwhelming compassion and goodwill towards all living beings. They are guides on a path to a better way of living, a guide to building the ancient Indian vision of *vasudhaiva kutumbakam* – the world as one family.

These ancient teachings have been painstakingly passed on from generation to generation with great care taken to preserve the sacred messages. Long before the internet, or the printing press, or even handwritten books or scrolls, the scriptures were passed on orally from teacher to student, often chanted for hours every day. To give you an idea, there are four major Vedas, and it is said each one takes twelve years to memorize. So a *Chaturvedi* would have sacrificed forty-eight years of his life to memorize this sacred knowledge. I think the greatest tribute we can pay to these great souls, who sacrificed so much for us to benefit from this knowledge, is to read their work sincerely. We live in uncertain times, and I believe that by drawing upon the wisdom of the great ones who came before us, we have an opportunity in our search for truth, meaning, and safety for all.

It has been an incredible blessing working on this book with Nicholas Sutton, who is both a friend and a trusted teacher of Hindu Dharma. Together, we carefully sifted through the ocean of Hindu sacred texts, gathering verses that inspired us, and that we felt would inspire you too. In truth, however, we cannot do justice through this short text to the enormous body of religious literature that Hinduism offers, but what I hope we can do is to provide you with a taste of the values the tradition embodies, and hope that we convey the crucial duty incumbent upon us to preserve and embody the principles of Sanatana Dharma.

These verses are not to be read as a newspaper article, or a popular magazine, but they are to be meditated upon carefully. Imagine you were in the presence of Shri Krishna, as he spoke the sacred words of the *Bhagavad Gita*, or standing before one of the sages of the *Upanishads* as they imparted the highest truths of reality to their students. Tradition says it is through the accumulation of great merit that one is fortunate enough to gain exposure to these great teachings. They are greater than any material treasure and if we receive them with humility, an open heart and absolute sincerity, we open ourselves to the possibility of personal transformation and most importantly, we can become the ideal vehicles for goodness.

As you go through the verses presented here, if you find something profound, try to absorb it. If there is a particular verse, which deeply resonates with you, perhaps you can memorize it in Sanskrit and allow it to become a part of your life. Little by little, verse by verse, we create the vibrations of these powerful ideas, which can only be positive for the world at large.

Reading the Hindu scriptures and coming into contact with beings that have been profoundly affected by Sanatana

Dharma has changed my life forever. The purpose of this book is to try to share some of the greatest treasures of the world's collective inheritance. The verses draw upon the ideas of ahimsa – the path of non-violence, dharma – the innate sense of right action, bhakti – the way of devotional love, and many other transformative ideas. By working with these verses, by exploring the scriptures they have been taken from, we can shift our outlook from the materialistic perspective of desire to looking at the world with love and compassion for every single living being. Carl Jung once said, "The whole world wants peace and the whole world prepares for war." However, I believe the ideal of peace can become a realistic possibility. We face challenges socially, between religious communities, environmentally, with the state of the global economy, and even psychologically, but to create the world of peace we all dream of, we will need to grasp the essence of the timeless teachings of Sanatana Dharma.

With Love,
Hanuman Dass

THE FOUNDATION OF HINDUISM

1. *The Mahābhārata* (3.281.34)

34. *adrohaḥ sarva-bhūteṣu karmaṇā manasā girā*
anugrahaś ca dānaṃ ca satāṃ dharmaḥ sanātanaḥ

Never displaying malice towards any living being through actions, thoughts or words; acts of kindness, and giving in charity; this is the Sanātana Dharma adhered to by righteous persons.

Many people in India do not like the name 'Hinduism', seeing it as a foreign imposition, and prefer to refer to their religion as 'Sanatana Dharma'. This literally means eternal or unchanging religious life. But what exactly does Sanatana Dharma entail? In this verse, the wise Savitri gives a threefold definition in her discussion of dharma with Yama, the God of Death, who is so delighted by her words that he grants renewed life to her dying husband. The definition of Sanatana Dharma she gives here is both negative and positive, not causing any harm to another being, and then performing acts of kindness and charity on behalf of others. Significantly, there is no demand here for any act of worship, or even faith in God, for the Sanatana Dharma is open to believers and non-believers alike.

CORE PRINCIPLES

2. *The Mahābhārata* (13.147.22)

22. *ahiṃsā satyam akrodho dānam etac catuṣṭayam*
ajāta-śatro sevasva dharma eṣa sanātanaḥ

Not harming, truthfulness, remaining free from anger, and charity, are the four practices you must adhere to, Ajātaśatru. This is the Sanātana Dharma.

In this verse, we have another delineation of Sanatana Dharma, this time given to King Yudhishthira by Bhishma, his sagacious grandfather, just before the latter decides to depart from this world. The definition given here is rather similar to that offered above by Savitri, including ahimsa, remaining free of anger, and giving gifts in charity. To these virtues, Bhishma also adds truthfulness, which can probably be taken as meaning honesty in all one's dealings. These are of course virtues that should be adhered to by all human beings, but they are also indicators of spiritual achievement. Spirituality is not some vague notion, or acts of obscure religiosity, but is very practical. The state of consciousness attained can best be measured by the extent to which one is willing and able to avoid harming and anger, to give frequently to those in need, and to be honest in all one's dealings. This is why the Sanatana Dharma is explained in this very practical way.

THE SUPERIOR UNDERSTANDING

3. *The Mahābhārata* 8.49.48-50

48. *duṣkaraṃ parama-jñānaṃ tarkeṇātra vyavasyati*
śrutir dharma iti hy eke vadanti bahavo janāḥ

49. *na tv etat pratisūyāmi na hi sarvaṃ vidhīyate*
prabhavārthāya bhūtānāṃ dharma-pravacanaṃ kṛtam

50. *dhāraṇād dharmam ity āhur dharmo dhārayati prajāḥ*
yaḥ syād dhāraṇa-saṃyuktaḥ sa dharma iti niścayaḥ

48. The superior understanding is hard to achieve, but one may be able to achieve this with determination and logic. Many persons, however, assert that it is the *śruti* (scripture) that defines dharma.

49. I do not reject this point of view, but not every case can be resolved in this way. The precepts of dharma have been set in place in order to allow living beings to flourish.

50. Hence, people conclude that dharma is based on the principle of sustenance, for dharma sustains living beings. Whatever may bring about the sustenance of living beings is therefore dharma; this must be the conclusion.

Even when the principles underlying dharma are established, it can be difficult to work out exactly how to implement them in any given situation. These verses directly address this issue. Krishna spoke these words to Arjuna on the battlefield, when Arjuna was facing a dilemma over whether he should strictly adhere to the principle of truthfulness, even when to do so would be harmful to other people. Krishna's reply is interesting and unequivocal. For many religious people, scripture provides a code of unbreakable rules that must be followed in all circumstances, but Krishna is not satisfied by this approach. He does not completely dismiss scripture (nor the power of human logic), but ultimately, he concludes that dharma is not a fixed code of conduct. Rather each situation should be taken on its own merits, with the crucial criterion being what is most beneficial to living beings. Honesty, intelligence, and integrity are required to reach a conclusion of this type, but ultimately, the good of all beings transcends any necessity imposed by scriptural injunction. That is Krishna's view.

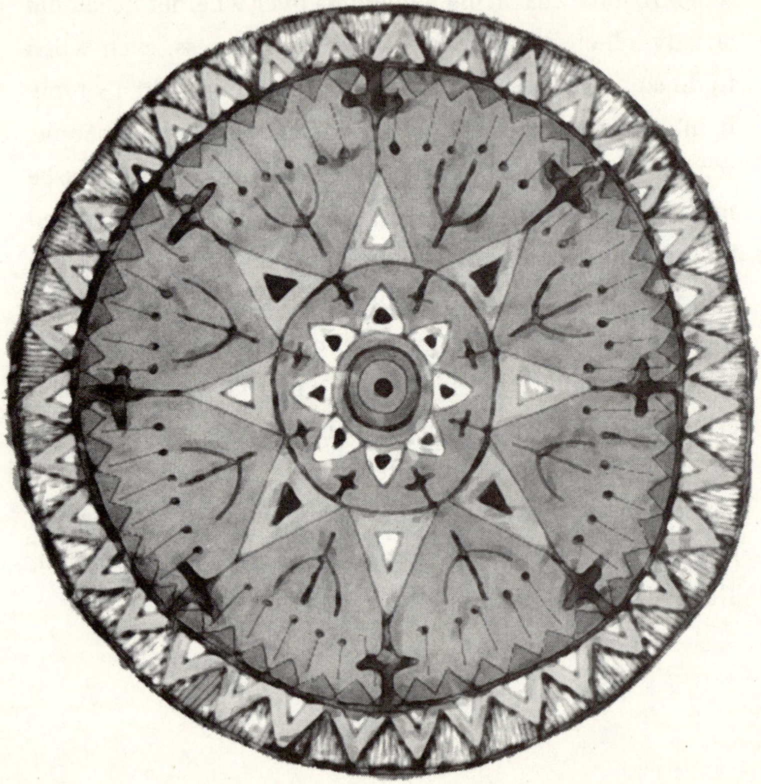

QUALITIES OF GOOD PEOPLE

4. *The Bhagavad Gītā* (16.1-3)

1. *śrī bhagavān uvāca*
abhayaṃ sattva-saṃśuddhir jñāna-yoga-vyavasthitiḥ
dānaṃ damaś ca yajñaś ca svādyāyas tapa ārjavam

2. *ahiṃsā satyam akrodhas tyāgaḥ śāntir apaiśunam*
dayā bhūteṣv aloluptvaṃ mārdavaṃ hrīr acāpalam

3. *tejaḥ kṣamā dhṛtiḥ śaucam adroho nātimānitā*
bhavanti saṃpadaṃ daivīm abhijātasya bhārata

1. Fearlessness, being pure at heart, remaining resolute in the pursuit of knowledge through Yoga practice, charity, self-control, performing sacrifices, study of the Vedas, austerity, honesty.

2. Not harming, truthfulness, avoiding anger, renunciation, tranquility, never maligning others, compassion for other beings, remaining free of greed; kindness, modesty, never wavering.

3. Energy, patience, resolve, purity, the absence of malice and of arrogance; these constitute the qualities of one born with the godly disposition, Bhārata.

In the sixteenth chapter of *the Bhagavad Gita*, Krishna outlines the disposition of those who are godly by nature, and those who display the opposite characteristics. In these opening three verses of the chapter, he lists the qualities and modes of conduct of those whose disposition is godly, and I think we can regard this as a further discourse on the true nature of Sanatana Dharma. Many of these qualities can be recognized from the passages given above, but it is interesting to note that in this case religious and spiritual behaviour is added. Hence, we can observe the advocacy of ritual acts of worship, and of dedication to the practice of Yoga meditation. In this way, the concept of Sanatana Dharma is broadened further, although the essential elements of not harming, compassion for all beings, and giving charity, remain clearly to the fore.

LOVE EVERYBODY

5. *The Mahābhārata* (12.251.24)

sarvam priyābhyupagataṃ dharmam āhur manīṣiṇaḥ
paśyaitam lakṣaṇād deśaṃ dharmādharme yudhiṣṭhira

The wise say that dharma is whatever is based on love for all beings. This is the characteristic mark that distinguishes dharma from *adharma*, Yudhishthira.

Bhishma gives a definition of dharma that shows clearly that it is not merely a matter of following designated rules, as laid down in some texts. Rather, dharma is a reflection of one's consciousness. 'Love for all beings' might sound a rather glib phrase, but what it means is that one has transcended narrow self-interest, and come to realize the unity of all existence. This may be as a single creation of the deity, or as the oneness of Brahman, but in all cases, dharma and spiritual realization are intimately related. To have love for all beings, one must develop a mood of absolute compassion in which one cannot tolerate the suffering of others. One then takes whatever action is possible to alleviate that suffering, and it is this form of action that is designated as dharma. Again we see that the exact form of action to be adopted is left to the intelligence of the individual, but the principle of universal love is immovable and absolute.

COMPASSION

6. *The Mahābhārata* (13.5.23)

23. *anukrośo hi sādhūnāṃ su-mahad-dharma-lakṣaṇam*
anukrośaś ca sādhūnāṃ sadā prītiṃ prayacchati

Amongst righteous persons, compassion is the great characteristic mark of dharma and compassion is always a source of delight for the righteous.

This is another verse from Bhishma's teachings on dharma, given to Yudhishthira towards the end of the *Mahabharata*. In this case, it is the quality of compassion that receives the greatest emphasis, being designated as the lakshana, or characteristic quality, that reveals an action, speech, or thought, to be a manifestation of the Sanatana Dharma. By compassion, Bhishma means that sense of sympathy and absolute good will towards other living beings, so that a person cannot bear to see them suffer. In one sense, this is a moral attribute, but it is also a deeply spiritual quality, and this attitude of absolute compassion for all beings is the only true indicator of genuine spirituality. It is possible to imitate the characteristics of spiritual persons in many ways, but genuine compassion must take on a practical manifestation, always being willing to give up time and wealth to those who are in need.

NON-HARMING

7. *The Mahābhārata* (12.254.16-17)

16. *yadā cāyaṃ na bibheti yadā cāsmān na bibhyeti*
yadā necchati na dveṣṭi tadā sidhyati vai dvijaḥ

17. *yadā na kurute bhāvaṃ sarva-bhūteṣu pāpakam*
karmaṇā manasā vācā brahma saṃpadyate tadā

16. When a Brahmin no longer has any fear, when no fear arises because of him, and when he feels neither desire nor loathing, he has certainly achieved success.

17. When he is never the cause of any harmful condition for any living being with his actions, thoughts, or words, then he has realized Brahman.

In this passage from the *Mahabharata*, Bhishma is citing the words of the noble Tuladhara in support of the view that proper conduct will always be guided by the core value of not causing harm to anyone. In fact, Tuladhara is particularly referring to priests who kill animals for meat offerings as a part of the Vedic ritual. No human being or creature need fear the truly awakened person, for his attitude towards every living entity is utterly benign. This applies not just to his actions, which are instinctively sympathetic, but to his words and thoughts as well. The point is clearly made that not harming is not simply an ethical ordinance, but is the only true indication of spiritual awakening. Only when this outlook on the world is displayed can a person be recognized as truly spiritually awakened.

KINDNESS TO ALL

8. *The Mahābhārata* (14.46.17-18)

17. *gṛhastho brahmacārī ca vānaprastho 'tha vā punaḥ*
ya icchen mokṣam āsthātum uttamāṃ vṛttim āśrayet

18. *abhayaṃ sarva-bhūtebhyo dattvā naiṣkarmyam ācaret*
sarva-bhūta-hito maitraḥ sarvendriya-yato muniḥ

17. Whether he is a householder, unmarried student, or retired to the forest, anyone who wishes to achieve liberation from rebirth must adhere to the perfect way of life.

18. Only when he bestows the gift of fearlessness on all living beings can the sage achieve freedom from karma. He should act for the welfare of all beings, show kindness to all, and bring his senses under control.

This passage is taken from a section of the *Mahabharata* known as the Anugita, in which Krishna teaches Arjuna further as a supplement to the better known *Bhagavad Gita*, which appears earlier in the *Mahabharata*. Here we can observe the connection made between a life based on dharma, characterized by service to others, and the spiritual quest for higher realization and liberation from rebirth. Hence, this pursuit of dharma in the form of not harming and compassion for all beings is both a moral precept and an essential part of the spiritual endeavour.

TULADHARA'S RULE OF LIFE

9. *The Mahābhārata* (12.254.6)

6. *adroheṇaiva bhūtānām alpa-droheṇa vā punaḥ*
yā vṛttiḥ sa paro dharmas tena jīvāmi jājale

6. Causing no harm to any living being, or at least as little harm as possible, is the way of life that represents the highest expression of dharma. That is the rule by which I live, Jājali.

This is another verse from Tuladhara, who is cited by Bhishma as a devoted adherent of the highest expression of dharma. The phrase used here is *paro dharma*, meaning the highest expression of dharma, and again this is defined as a form of lifestyle in which no harm is caused to any living being. If we think carefully about it, this principle can be applied to all aspects of our lives, our vocation, our diet, our relationships, the way we interact with others, the words we speak, and even the thoughts we think. If we are attempting to pursue a life based on the highest expression of dharma, then all of these should be undertaken based on the precept of never causing harm or distress to others.

THE MARK OF DHARMA

10. *The Mahābhārata* (14.43.19)

19. *ata ūrdhvaṃ pravakṣyāmi niyataṃ dharma-lakṣaṇam*
ahiṃsā lakṣaṇo dharmo hiṃsā cādharma-lakṣaṇā

19. Now, I will speak about what is established as the characteristic mark of dharma. Ahiṃsā is the characteristic mark of dharma, whilst Hiṃsā is characteristic of *adharma.*

The determining of what course of action is best is often very difficult, as at times it can seem that the available possibilities have both positive and negative attributes. Some help in decision-making is given by the advice offered in this verse, namely that in all cases ahimsa should be the crucial criterion to employ. Ahimsa literally means 'not harming', and naturally has both active and passive applications. For example, if I walk past a lake and see a child drowning, I might refuse to help because I am wearing a brand new pair of trousers that I do not want to spoil. In that case, I have not harmed the child directly, but nonetheless my refraining from active intervention must be regarded as a breach of the principle of ahimsa. So, when I decide on the most appropriate, or dharmic, course of action, this is always the test; what course of conduct best meets the criterion of ahimsa by freeing others from distress. Of course, we are not all saints, and at times all of us will fall short of that absolute standard. The important thing is that we are aware of the ideal, and try to live up to it as far as we are able to do so.

CRUELTY

11. *The Mahābhārata* (13.117.10-11)

10. *sva-māṃsaṃ para-māṃsair yo vivardhayitum icchati*
nāsti kṣudrataras tasmān na nṛśamsataro naraḥ

11. *na hi prāṇāt priyataraṃ loke kiṃcana vidyate*
tasmād dayāṃ naraḥ kuryād yathātmani tathā pare

10. There is no one crueler than that person who seeks to strengthen his own flesh by means of the flesh of another creature, and no one who is more malicious.

11. There is nothing in the world dearer than one's life. Therefore, a man should show compassion towards others, as he would have others behave towards himself.

Whenever the idea of ahimsa is discussed, it naturally gives rise to consideration of the dharmic diet. Should we eat meat, or even eggs and dairy products? To do so can be regarded as an infringement of the principle of ahimsa, but at the same time, an overly evangelical attitude on issues of this type is rarely conducive. Each individual must decide for himself or herself, and condemnation of others' conduct is not a desirable approach to take. For the *Mahabharata*, however, the issue is one on which it is overtly forthright. The simple moral equation is posited: Is it acceptable to seek pleasure through action that causes suffering to other beings? All of us love life more dearly than any other possession and so depriving an animal of life must cause it to suffer distress. Few, if any of us, need to eat meat to maintain our lives or good health, and the motive for doing so is therefore simply one of taste and desire. When it is couched in these terms, the answer to the question posed above does seem to be rather obvious.

AVOIDING MEAT

12. *The Mahābhārata* (13.116.31)

yasmād grasati caivāyur hiṃsakānāṃ mahā-dyute
tasmād vivarjayen māṃsaṃ ya icched bhūtim ātmanaḥ

Because the lifespan of those who injure others is reduced, O effulgent one, one who seeks his own prosperity must completely abstain from eating meat.

A further reason given in the *Mahabharata* for avoiding meat is practical rather than ethical: to do so shortens one's own life. It is not entirely clear whether this idea is based on medical science, or on the notion of karmic reaction, but given that it is *himsakas*, persons who harm, who are being spoken of, the latter interpretation seems more likely. In either case, however, the argument stands. Statistics demonstrate that those who follow a vegetarian diet generally live longer lives than those who eat meat (although this could be because vegetarians tend to be more careful about eating healthy food). And the doctrine of karma dictates that one's own actions produce a positive or negative reaction in the form of enjoyment or suffering, either in this or in a future life. According to the rule of karma, the cutting short of the life of another living being is likely to produce a similar effect on one's own existence.

THE KARMA OF EATING

13. *The Mahābhārata* (13.116.37)

37. *yo hi khādati māṃsāni prāṇināṃ jīvitārthinām*
hatānāṃ vā mṛtānāṃ vā yathā hantā tathaiva saḥ

37. Regardless of whether or not he afflicted or killed the creature himself, anyone who consumes the flesh of living beings, which all have a desire to sustain their lives, is to be regarded as their killer.

In the debate over a vegetarian or non-vegetarian diet, some may feel that they are not culpable because they do not directly perform the action of killing. The slaughterman alone must take the karma and consequences for killing the animal. Here though this expectation is refuted, it is only because people desire to eat the flesh of an animal that the slaughterman performs his grisly task; those people are therefore equally culpable, and will suffer karmic consequences for the direct action performed.

NOBLE ASPIRATIONS

14. *Rig Veda Samhitā* (1.89.1)

ā no bhadrāḥ kratavo yantu viśvataḥ

Let noble aspirations come from all directions.

This short aphorism from the *Rigveda Samhita* (the hymn portion of the *Rigveda*) is very simple and yet highly profound. It is in essence a prayer for personal improvement. We have many hopes and aspirations in life, but some of these may be based on greed or selfish desire. The prayer here is that the hopes we nurture will all be noble ones that do no harm to any being, and which are for the benefit of the world. I am sure the life experiences of all of us clearly reveal what is meant here.

TRUE HAPPINESS

15. *Vālmīki Rāmāyaṇa* (3.9.30-31)

30. *dharmād arthaḥ prabhavati dharmāt prabhavate sukham*
dharmeṇa labhate sarvaṃ dharma-sāram idaṃ jagat

31. *ātmānaṃ niyamais tais taiḥ karṣayitvā prayatnataḥ*
prāpyate nipuṇair dharmo na sukhāl labhate sukham

30. Prosperity arises from dharma; happiness arises from dharma. A person can achieve all things through dharma; dharma is the very essence of this world.

31. Making themselves emaciated by the diligent practice of various restraints, those who are skilled in such practice achieve the state of dharma. Happiness is never achieved simply through the pursuit of pleasure.

In this passage, we return to the subject of dharma, but now from the perspective of the *Ramayana*, as it presents words of instruction spoken by Sita to Rama. The idea of a wife giving instruction on dharma to her husband is interesting in itself, but particular attention should be paid to the wisdom she imparts. First, she insists that satisfaction in this world comes not from the fulfilment of selfish desire, but from adherence to a life of dharma. If we wish to find happiness and success in life then dharma is the key, and never greed or aggression. Many people pursue selfish goals, and I am sure that would include each one of us, but the real pleasure in life is derived from the virtues of compassion, giving freely, and rendering service to those in need.

TRUTH

16. *Vālmīki Rāmāyaṇa* (2.109.12-13)

12. *udvijante yathā sarpān narād anṛta-vādinaḥ*
dharmaḥ satya-paro loke mūlaṃ sarvasya cocyate

13. *satyam eveśvaro loke satye dharmaḥ sadāśritaḥ*
satya-mūlāni sarvāṇi satyān nāsti paraṃ padam

12. People recoil from a man whose words are false just as they do from a snake. Dharma has its basis in truth; truth is said to be the root of all things.

13. Truth alone is the Lord in this world for dharma always resides in truth. Truth is the root of everything; there is nothing that has a higher status than truth.

Here Valmiki cites the words of Rama himself, who is addressing the sage Jajali. For Rama, truth is the essence of dharma, and by that I think we should take him to mean honesty and integrity in all our dealings, rather than just speaking veracious words. We have already seen how Sanatana Dharma is based on principle rather than strict precept so that each individual must decide on the best course of conduct to pursue in each situation. To do this requires both intelligence and integrity, for it is all too easy to convince oneself that the course of action one would like to follow is also the one that is right and proper. Moreover, whether it is in private or professional affairs, the truthful person should always be true to his or her word in a manner that can be relied on. Again, this ideal is far easier to postulate than to do adhere to at all times. However, it is an ideal to be kept constantly in mind; it is the example that Rama himself has set for us, as revealed by the words of the Ramayana.

BAD KARMA

17. *Vālmīki Rāmāyaṇa* (3.29.9)

9. *na-cirāt prāpyate loke pāpānāṃ karmaṇāṃ phalam*
sa-viṣāṇām ivānnānāṃ bhuktānāṃ kṣaṇad-ācara

9. In this world the results of wicked deeds very soon afflict the performer, just as poisoned food quickly has an effect on one who eats it, O you who roam at night.

This verse forms a part of a speech made by Rama to Khara, the *rakshasa* commander of Ravana's army. Having attacked Rama and Lakshmana, Khara has been defeated, and is distressed. The point Rama makes is one that can be either taken as a statement of the doctrine of karma, or as a simple assertion based on observation of the ways of the world. The law of karma dictates that wicked deeds such as aggression against others must bring future suffering to the performer, and if the verse is taken in this sense, then it indicates that negative karma is experienced very quickly, as well as in future births. However, those who seek personal gain through actions that harm others rarely find satisfaction in life. People despise them and they make enemies who in time act against them. Hence, even without reference to the doctrine of karma, we can see that aggression against others is rarely the pathway to any form of meaningful success in life.

GREED

18. *Bhāgavata Purāṇa* (7.15.20)

kāmasyāntaṃ ca kṣut-tṛḍbyāṃ krodhasyaitat phalodayāt
jano yāti na lobhasya jitvā bhuktvā diśo bhuvaḥ

Hunger and thirst end for one who eats and drinks, anger calms when the right result is achieved, but even by conquering and enjoying all the directions of the world, a person does not find any end to his greed.

This is a verse from Book Seven of the *Bhagavata*, in which the sage Narada gives extensive instruction to King Yudhishthira. The desires we hold in this world, as well any anger or irritation we feel, will generally run their course, but greed is something that will never diminish simply by feeding its cravings. The person beset by greed constantly wants more wealth and more possessions, and however much these longings are fulfilled, the sense of desire is never satisfied. How else can we explain how it is that the wealthiest persons in the world still devote themselves to greater and greater accumulation? In fact, the more a person gains, well beyond all possible requirements, the more this burning sense of greed increases. Hence, attempting to satisfy our desire for gain by accumulating wealth is like putting more fuel onto a blazing fire. Greed must be restrained, as it is the great obstacle to dharma, but this will never be achieved by seeking to fulfil our constant cravings.

THE RIGHT VERSUS THE PLEASURABLE

19. *Kaṭha Upaniṣad* (2.1)

anyac chreyo 'nyad utaiva preyas te ubhe nānārthe puruṣam sinītaḥ
tayoḥ śreya ādadānasya sādhu bhavate hīyate'rthād ya u preyo vṛṇīte

(Mrityu said) There is a clear distinction between the righteous and the pleasurable. They have different purposes. Of the two, it is good for the one who holds on to the righteous choice; the one who seeks only the pleasurable will not achieve the goal.

Here is a well-known verse from the *Katha Upanishad* in which Mrityu, the God of Death, instructs the blessed Nachiketas. The latter has asked Mrityu to reveal to him the secrets of the afterlife, and because of the significance of this inquiry, the god tests his interlocutor by offering him all manner of material pleasures instead. Nachiketas, however, is resolute in seeking only higher knowledge, and it is when his qualities thus become apparent that Mrityu speaks this verse. Although it is specific to this situation, the idea here has much wider implications that affect all our lives. In so many situations, we find ourselves having to make choices between the course of action that pleases us and an alternative we perceive to be more dharmic or more in line with pure virtue. Here the former is referred to as *preyas* and the latter as *shreyas*. Sometimes, we can convince ourselves that what we want to do is actually morally correct, running the specious arguments through our minds, but this is where the truthfulness spoken of by Rama comes into play. There is no need to feel guilty if we choose the pleasing option, we all do this at various times, but as far as possible we should strive to follow the righteous course just a little more when such situations arise.

A MESSAGE FOR STUDENTS

20. *Taittirīya Upaniṣad* (1.11.1-2)

1. *vedam anūcyācāryo'ntevāsinam anuśāsti; satyaṃ vada; dharmaṃ cara; svādhyāyān mā pramadaḥ; ācāryāya priyaṃ dhanam āhṛtya prajātantum mā vyavacchetsīḥ; satyān na pramaditavyam; dharmān na pramaditavyam; kuśalān na pramaditavyam; bhūtyai na pramadityavyam; svādhyāya-pravacanābhyām na pramaditavyam.*

2. *deva-pitṛ-kāryābhyāṃ na pramaditavyam; mātṛ-devo bhava; pitṛ-devo bhava; ācārya-devo bhava; atithi-devo bhava; yāny anavadyāni karmāṇi tāni sevitavyāni; no itarāṇi; yāny asmākaṃ sucaritāni; tāni tvayopāsyāni; no itarāṇi.*

1. Having taught the Veda, the teacher instructs the student. "Speak what is true. Practise dharma. Do not neglect your recital of the Veda. Having given generously to your teachers, do not cut off the thread of offspring. Let there be no neglect of truth. Let there be no neglect of the various forms of dharma. Let there be no neglect of prosperity. Especially, let there be no neglect of the study and public recitation of the Veda. Let there be no neglect of duties to the gods and ancestors.

2. Treat your mother as a god. Treat your father as a god. Treat your teacher as a god. Treat your guests as gods. Whatever good practices there are in the world, you should do those and no others.

The first part of this passage from the *Taittiriya Upanishad* consists of general instruction that a teacher gives his student when the latter has completed his studies. The second verse, however, gives important insight into another facet of dharma, namely the respect, and care for parents and, in fact, all the elders that we have a relationship with. In the modern world, it is increasingly difficult for people to give up their limited time and resources in order to care for or provide company for parents and other elders, but dharma dictates that we should always strive to do a little more than we are at present. This is the nature of dharma; few if any of us can live the perfect dharmic life, but we can all move just a little closer to that ideal.

THE MOTHER

21. *The Mahābhārata* (13.108.14-15)

14. *daśācāryānupādhyāya apādhyāyān pitā daśa*
daśa chaiva pitṛn mātā sarvām vā pṛthivīm api

15. *gauraveṇābhibhavati nāsti mātṛ-samo guruḥ*
mātā garīyasī yac ca tenaitāṃ manyate janaḥ

14. Worth ten scholars is the teacher, worth ten teachers is the father, worth ten fathers is the mother. Indeed the mother is worth more than the Earth.

15. There is no guru greater than the mother, who surpasses all others in her ability to perform the role of a teacher. Every person regards his mother as superior to all.

This passage from the *Mahabharata* is interesting because of the way in which it insists that the mother should be respected above all others, even more than the father. Indian culture and Indian religion is often accused of being demeaning to women, and with some justification, but here we see the *Mahabharata* offering a radically alternative point of view. The mother should be like a goddess for all sons and daughters, to be revered, cared for, and in some way worshipped. Her wishes should be acknowledged and as far as possible acted upon, for reverence for elders and the mother in particular, is an essential feature of dharma, fully in line with the values of non-harming and compassion we have noted already.

THE SKY AND THE EARTH

22. *Rig Veda Saṃhitā* (6.70.6)

ūrjaṃ no dyauś ca pṛthivī ca pinvatām pitā mātā viśva-vidā sudaṃsasā

saṃrarāṇe rodasī viśva-śambhuvā saniṃ vājiṃ rayim asme saminvatām

May the sky and earth, the all-knowing mother and father, nourish us with plentiful food through their wonderful deeds.

May both together, working in union for the benefit of all, proceed forward to grant wealth, strength, and prosperity.

The *Rigveda* here gives one obvious reason why concern for parents' well-being should be such a prominent feature of the Sanatana Dharma. In our younger days, we are completely dependent on our mother and father for everything we need in life, and we are nurtured and sustained by the constant love they show for us. Later in life, our parents are often in need of our care, attention, and love and acknowledging this responsibility can be regarded as a form of gratitude. Again, one can only accept this dharma according to one's capacity, but it is something that should be kept in mind, so that we try to do a little more than we do at present. Of course, some parents may not be worthy recipients of our attention, and it may be better to dissociate ourselves from them; the well-known story of Prahrada reveals a clear example of this, but such instances are rare.

LONGING AND SEPARATION

23. *Rāmacharitamānasa* (*Sundara-khaṇḍa*, 14.1-4)

1. *kaheu rāma biyoga tava sītā mo kartuṃ sakala bhae biparītā*
nava taru kisalaya manahu kṛsānū kāla nisā sama nisi sasi bhānū

2. *kubalayabipina kuṃtabana sarisā bārida tapata tela janu barisā*
je hita rahe karata tei pīrā uraga svāsa sama tribidha samīrā

3. *kahehū teṃ kacchu dukha ghaṭi hoi kāhi kahauṃ yeha jāna na koi tatva prema kara mama aru torā jānata priyā eku manu morā*

4. *so manu sadā rahata tohi pāhīṃ jānu prītirasu etan ehi māhīṃ*
prabhusaṃdesu sonata baidehī magana prema tana sudhi nahi tehī

1. These are Rama's words: "Separation from you, Sītā, has turned my world upside down. The fresh and tender

leaves upon the trees are like tongues of fire; the night appears as dreadful as the night of death, and the moon scorches like the sun.

2. Buds of lotuses are like a forest of spears, and rain clouds drop boiling oil. Those who were friendly before now add to my pain, and the winds, cool, gentle and fragrant, are like the breath of a serpent.

3. One's agony is assuaged a little by speaking of it, but to whom shall I tell of it? No one can understand it. None but my own soul knows the essence of such love as yours and mine, beloved.

4. And this, my soul, ever abides with you. Know this to be the essence of my love." As soon as Sita heard the message of her lord, she became so absorbed in love that she lost all consciousness of her body.

The *Ramacharitamanasa* is a retelling of the *Ramayana* story composed in the 16th century AD by the poet Tulsidas. He chose to write in Hindi rather than Sanskrit because he sought to make the *Ramayana* available to all people, rather than it being confined to the elite social groups, who had knowledge of Sanskrit. This passage reveals Rama's message to Sita, delivered by Hanuman after Ravana had kidnapped her. It shows that the way of dharma is not austere and detached, but must also embody the spirit of love that should ideally exist between husband and wife, and indeed between all family members. From the dharmic perspective, this love is not a negative emotion to be wholly transcended as a part of the spiritual quest, for it is often an impetus towards virtue and sacrifice. We give up our own desires for the sake of those we love and do what is pleasing to them. We have compassion for them and we will never do them harm; this is the spirit of dharma, as noted in our previous selections.

O GODDESS

24. *Devī-Māhātmya* (1.56-57 or 75-76 in some manuscripts)

56. *tvayaitad dhāryate viśvaṃ tvayaitat srjyate jagat*
tvayaitat pālyate devi tvam atsy ante ca sarvadā

57. *visṛṣṭau sṛṣṭi-rūpā tvaṃ sthiti-rūpā ca pālane*
tathā saṃhṛti-rūpānte jagato 'sya jagan-maye

56. You sustain the entire world, and it is created by you as well. It is you who protect this world, O Goddess, and at the end, you consume it entirely.

57. When creation takes place, you take the form of creation, and when this world has to be protected, you take the form of maintenance. Likewise, at the end of time you assume the form of destruction, for the universe exists within your form.

A frequent criticism made against religion in modern times is that it discriminates against women, and does not allow them equal status with men. There is certainly merit in this point of view, and Hinduism has also shown itself to be culpable in this regard. One of the criticisms frequently heard is that the representation of God is always as an all-powerful male figure, an image that perpetuates the social stereotype on which gender-based oppression is based. In this respect, however, Indian religion proves to be an exception, as it does have a well-established Shakta tradition that reveres the Supreme Deity in female form as the Great Goddess known as Durga or Kali. This passage is taken from the *Devi Mahatmya* of the *Markandeya Purana*, and reveals very clearly how the Goddess is regarded as standing above any other manifestation of the Deity. This theological understanding may not always translate into any higher status for women at a social level, but it certainly offers a valuable resource to be utilized by those enlightened teachers who seek social reform.

CASTE: BIRTH OR QUALITIES?

25. *The Mahābhārata* (12.182.8)

8. *śūdre caitad bhavel lakṣyaṃ dvije caitan na vidyate*
na vai śūdro bhavec chūdro brāhmaṇo na ca brāhmaṇaḥ

8. If the marks of a Brahmin, described above, are found in a śūdra, or are not found in a Brahmin, then the person born as a śūdra is certainly not a śūdra, and the person born as a Brahmin is not a Brahmin.

Another area of concern in Indian society is the caste system, and in particular, the manner in which discrimination and oppression has often been the lot of those deemed to be of lower birth. Happily, the situation has improved significantly over the past hundred years, but there is still a long way to go before the egalitarian ideal is realized. One factor in this debate is whether one's caste status is determined by birth or by qualities, although in practice, it is generally birth alone that defines a person's caste identity. Here, however, the sage Bharadvaja gives a different opinion, relating to the earlier fourfold division of society into classes or *varnas*. We might also note that previously in the *Mahabharata*, Yudhishthira presents the same verse in his discussion with Nahusha. The view of these two famous teachers of dharma is that one's social status is determined only by one's qualities and disposition, and not by birth alone, thereby posing a challenge to the prevailing norms of Indian society. One may be proud of one's status as a Brahmin, but the teaching here is that birth in a Brahmin family is insufficient to guarantee that status, and it could be argued that this same sense of pride is enough to indicate that that person falls short of the standard demanded of a Brahmin.

REVERENCE FOR COWS

26. *The Mahābhārata* (13.77.5-6)

5. *gāvaḥ surabhi-gandhinyas tathā guggulu-gandhikā*
gāvaḥ pratiṣṭhā bhūtānāṃ gāvaḥ svastyanaṃ mahat

6. *gāvo bhūtaṃ bhaviṣyac ca gāvaḥ puṣṭiḥ sanātanī*
gāvo lakṣmyās tathā mūlaṃ goṣu dattaṃ na naśyati
annaṃ hi satataṃ gāvo devānāṃ paramaṃ haviḥ

5. Cows are always fragrant with the sweet aroma of the Guggulu perfume. Cows are the foundation for all living beings, and cows are supremely auspicious.

6. Cows are the past and the future; cows represent constant well-being; cows are the basis of prosperity, and the benefit of charity given for the sake of cows is never lost. Cows are a constant source of nourishment, and provide the best offerings for the gods.

One thing most people know about Hindus is that they show reverence for the cow, but few really understand the reason for this, and as a result, it has been ridiculed at times, with 'sacred cow' being used as a metaphor for any object or idea that is pointlessly respected. On a number of occasions, the *Mahabharata* emphasizes the view that cows should be respected, and even worshipped, and here some of the reasoning behind this custom is explained. Like one's parents, the cow provides human beings with food in the form of milk and dairy products, and so it is natural that one should reciprocate this bounty by showing respect, and providing for the well-being of the giver. Too often in the western world, animals are treated purely as a resource, to be exploited as fully as possible, but here we get a different perspective based on reciprocation rather than one-sided exploitation. At a broader level, one can apply this same mood of reciprocation to the whole of the natural world, and in India the Earth is often represented in the form of a cow. We ruthlessly exploit the resources of the Earth, to the point of causing harm to the environment and hence to our own well-being. If we could only learn the lesson revealed by the Hindu devotion to the cow, then perhaps our world would be a more wholesome place to inhabit.

BE LIKE TREES

27. *Bhāgavata Purāṇa* (10.22.32-35)

32. *paṣyataitān mahā-bhāgān parārthaikānta jīvitān*
vāta-varṣātapa-himān sahanto vārayanti naḥ

33. *aho eṣāṃ varaṃ janma sarva-prāny-upajīvanam*
su-janasyeva yeṣām vai vimukhā yānti nārthinaḥ

34. *patra-puṣpa-phala-cchāyā-mūla-valkala-dārubhiḥ*
gandha-niryāsa-bhasmāsthi-tokmaiḥ kāmān vitanvate

35. *etāvaj janma sāphalyam dehinām iha dehiṣu*
prāṇair arthair dhiyā vācā śreya-ācaraṇam sadā

32. Look at these fortunate trees. They live solely for the benefit of others. They tolerate wind, rain, heat, and snow, but still provide shelter for our benefit.

33. O how special is this birth as these trees, which bring life to all other beings. They are like the great persons of this world, for those in need never go away from them disappointed.

34. With their leaves, flowers, fruits, shade, roots, bark, and wood, as well as their scents, sap, ash, nuts, and shoots, they fulfil people's wishes.

35. Whether it be through life, wealth, words, or wisdom, a fruitful life is one that is beneficial to other beings, always endeavouring for their welfare.

Here is a passage from the *Bhagavata* in which the women of Vrindaban open up their hearts as they wander through the forest searching for Krishna. The point here, however, is the continuation of the idea discussed above concerning respect and reciprocation with regard to the natural world. These young women fully appreciate the debt of gratitude they owe to the trees that provide them with fruit, flowers, nuts, and fuel, and see this in relation to the idea of pure dharma. Just as we recognize the virtue of any person who is bountiful, kind, and giving, so we should see the natural world in the same way, and fully appreciate how much we owe to it for the things that are truly good in life.

WATERS!

28. *Rig Veda Saṃhitā* (10.9.1-2)

āpo hi ṣṭhā mayobhuvas tā na ūrje dadhātana mahe ranāya cakṣase
yo vaḥ śivatamo rasas tasya bhājayateha naḥ uśatīr iva mātaraḥ

Waters! You bring us the nourishing life force. Help us to find energy so that we may see delight. Let us share in your delightful provision, which you keep like a loving mother.

A similar point is made here in relation to the waters that flow in streams and rivers across the land. Too often, we see the fresh water polluted with chemicals or refuse, in a manner that shows a lack of respect for the natural world on which our lives depend. This hymn from the *Rigveda* displays both reverence for the waters as a source of life, and a sense of delight in the purity of their flow. Again, this is a feature of dharma that we would do well to follow today.

WHO REALLY KNOWS?

29. *Rig Veda Saṃhitā* (10.129.6-7)

6. *ko addhā veda ka iha pra vocat kuta ājātā kuta iyaṃ visṛṣṭiḥ arvāg devā asya visarjanenātha ko veda yata ābabhūva*

7. *iyaṃ visṛṣṭir yata ābabhūva yadi vā dadhe yadi vā na yo asyādhyakṣaḥ parame vyomantso āṇga veda yadi vā na veda*

6. Who really knows? Who here will proclaim it? Whence was it produced? From whence did creation emerge? The gods came afterwards, with the forming of the universe. So who really knows how it all began?

7. That out of which creation has arisen, whether it held it firm or did not, he who surveys it in the highest heaven, he surely knows it – or perhaps he does not.

Religion will usually claim to have access to knowledge of the world, and knowledge of proper moral conduct, because it has access to sources of truth that are revealed from a higher domain. Scripture is the obvious example, and it is frequently claimed that scriptural revelation can transcend human reason. This idea does give us a sense of certainty in an uncertain world, but at the same time, it can lead to dogmatism, and intolerance of other views. Too often religion has allowed this certainty to become a source of bigotry, and even a justification for the persecution of 'non-believers'. This passage is from the *Nasadiya Sukta,* one of the hymns of the tenth book of the *Rigveda Samhita,* and here we can observe a rather different approach from scripture. The truth is not so simple that it can be reduced to some short creed, for 'knowing' is very hard to achieve. The tone here is agnostic, which allows the reader to begin the spiritual quest, rather than concluding it with a single sentence. The lack of absolutism also leads inevitably to a mood of tolerance, and acceptance of other views, which again should be a salient feature of Sanatana Dharma.

ACT AS YOU SEE FIT

30. *The Bhagavad Gītā* (18.63)

63. *iti te jñānam ākhyātaṃ guhyād guhyataraṃ mayā*
vimṛśyaitad aśeṣeṇa yathecchasi tathā kuru

63. I have now revealed to you the wisdom that is the deepest of all mysteries. After fully considering what you have heard, you should then act as you see fit.

A similar point of view is encountered here at the end of the *Bhagavad Gita,* when Krishna has virtually concluded his teachings. He emphasizes the profound nature of the wisdom he has revealed, but he does not say to Arjuna, "And now you must obey and do exactly what I say." Rather, he encourages him to think deeply about the teachings, to reflect on their full significance, and then to reach his own conclusions. This is a startlingly different religious approach, which accepts and allows for the integrity and intelligence of those who study the scripture. The text is not dictating a dogmatic creed, but rather offering vital assistance for the spiritual quest to those with ears to listen. And of course, this non-dogmatic approach to religion fosters the mood of tolerance and diversity that is a feature of Indian religion at its best. Each person must pursue his or her own spiritual quest, and the scriptures are friends, helpers, and guides, not domineering masters who demand absolute submission.

DEDICATION TO GOD

31. *The Bhagavad Gītā* (4.11)

11. *ye yathā māṃ prapadyante tāṃs tathaiva bhajāmy aham*
mama vartmānuvartante manuṣyāḥ pārtha sarvaśaḥ

11. According to the manner in which they dedicate themselves to me, so I devote myself to them. In all circumstances, Pārtha, people are pursuing my path.

This is a well-known verse from the *Gita* that is rightly acknowledged as a celebration of diversity. We all have a tendency to desire superiority over others in some field or other and this sentiment can be a great barrier to the pursuit of dharma. Where religion is concerned, we may claim that our faith is the only right one and that therefore I am a part of the elite group of the 'saved'. Those who do not share my beliefs must be inferior, or even the enemies of God, because they do not accept the true doctrine. Here Krishna offers a radically different perspective, indicating that different forms of religion exist because of the differing spiritual needs of different people. That does not mean that everything done in the name of religion must be accepted, as some clearly violate the core precepts of dharma, but where matters of doctrine are concerned, we should not be overly dogmatic or condemn those who do not share our own beliefs. As long as it does not oppose the core precepts of dharma, every person's religious belief should be accepted and embraced, not merely tolerated, for that is the true spirit of ahimsa, the essence of dharma.

OM!

32. *Māṇḍukya Upaniṣad*, (1)

om ity etad akṣaram idaṃ sarvaṃ tasyopavyākhyānaṃ bhūtaṃ bhavad bhaviṣyad iti sarvam oṃkāra eva, yac cānyat trikālātītaṃ tad apy oṃkāra eva

Om! All this world is that syllable. Here is a further explanation of it: past, present, and future are all merely the syllable Om. Moreover, whatever else there might be beyond these three phases of time is also just Om.

Now we move on to matters of pure spirituality. In India, the sound vibration Om has for centuries been regarded as the most sacred of all mantras, and here the *Mandukya Upanishad* clearly equates the mantra with the philosophical notion of Brahman. In Upanishadic thought, everything that exists is Brahman alone, and in this passage the same is said of Om. The whole world, past, present, and future, is nothing but Brahman and because Om is the sound that is Brahman, everything that is real is Om. Hence, the proper vibration of the sound of Om brings one into direct contact with the supreme reality, and thereby helps with spiritual awakening.

REINCARNATION

33. *The Bhagavad Gītā* (2.22)

vāsāṃsi jīrṇāni yathā vihāya navāni gṛhṇāti naro 'parāṇi
tathā śarīrāṇi vihāya jīrṇāny anyāni saṃyāti navāni dehī

Just as a man casts aside old clothes and puts on other ones that are new, so the embodied soul casts aside old bodies, and accepts other new ones.

In this verse, Krishna talks about the eternal soul in every living being, and the process of transmigration. This idea of reincarnation is shared by almost all schools of Indian thought, although Buddhism rejects the concept of the soul, and speaks instead of there being a chain of causation running from one bodily form to another. The *Gita*, however, stresses the idea of the eternal *atman*, which is held in bondage in this world, and which moves from one body to another, impelled by the force of past karma. Here the process of transmigration is compared to the changing of clothes, a simple metaphor that anyone can understand. What is perhaps less well understood is that the mental covering transmigrates with the *atman*, in the form of a subtle body, and it is in this way that past actions reshape the soul's future identity in a new bodily form. Past actions leave an impression on the mind and are therefore carried forward from one lifetime to another.

POLISH THE MIRROR

34. *Śvetāśvatara Upaniṣad* (2.14)

14. *yathaiva bimbaṃ mṛdayopaliptaṃ tejomayaṃ bhrājate tat sudhāntam*
tad vātma-tattvam prasamīkṣya dehī ekaḥ kṛtārtho bhavate vīta-śokaḥ

Just as a mirror covered in dust shines brightly when it has been cleaned, so the embodied being stands alone when he has realized the real nature of the self, his goal achieved, and free from suffering.

The *Upanishad* is speaking here about the notion of liberation from the conditions of the world. The flaws in our character are compared to dust on a mirror, which prevents it from properly revealing any reflected object. The process of Sanatana Dharma is one of cleansing, so that the higher qualities come to the fore, and the spiritual light of the soul shines more fully. Then the embodied entity, the *atman*, 'stands alone' in the sense that it begins to detach itself from its unwanted association with matter, and the suffering we must endure because of that association comes to an end. This liberation from the world comes through knowledge of our true spiritual nature, and this in turn is brought about through the cleansing power of Sanatana Dharma.

THE END OF SUFFERING

35. *Śvetāśvatara Upaniṣad* (6.20)

yadā carmavad ākāśaṃ veṣṭayiṣyanti mānavāḥ
tadā devam avijñāya duḥkhasyānto bhaviṣyati

Only when men are able to roll up space as if it were a leather mat will there be an end to suffering without knowledge of God.

It is interesting to note that in our previous verse knowledge of the self was presented as the means by which liberation from the world is achieved, whilst here it is knowledge of God. This clearly reflects the Indian view of the identity that exists between God, the created world, and each individual being. We try in many different ways to counteract the difficulties life presents us with, but none of the solutions we attempt is wholly satisfactory. Always some residual suffering will remain. The fully effective solution suggested here is that we try to transcend the world through spiritual means, to come to an awareness of the presence of the divine, both in our daily lives and pervading the entire created world. Only when this awakened consciousness is achieved can the problems of life be completely ameliorated. This is the view of the *Upanishad.*

AGE AFTER AGE

36. *The Bhagavad Gītā* (4.7-8)

yadā yadā hi dharmasya glānir bhavati bhārata
abhyuttānam adharmasya tadātmānaṃ srjāmy aham
paritrāṇāya sādhūnāṃ vināśāya ca duṣkṛtām
dharma-saṃsthāpanārthāya saṃbhavāmi yuge yuge

Whenever there is a decline in dharma, O Bharata, and whenever there is an increase in *adharma*, then I manifest myself.

For the protection of the righteous, for the destruction of wrongdoers, and for establishing dharma, I appear age after age.

These two verses, spoken by Krishna in the *Bhagavad Gita*, establish the doctrine of *avatara*, which has been fundamental to Indian understandings of the nature of God. The idea established here is that the Supreme Deity not only exists in his own spiritual domain, but also directly manifests his presence in the created world whenever it is required to ensure that dharma does not disappear, and that righteous persons can remain active. The stories of Krishna, Rama, Narasingha, and others, are all based on this idea, as they tell of the activities in this world of these manifestations of God. Moreover, many believe that great teachers of religion in all parts of the world reflect the doctrine of *avatara* so that for Hindus the idea of the divinity of Christ is very easy to accept, whilst the Buddha is widely acknowledged as being inspired by his own inner divinity.

DO YOU KNOW BRAHMAN?

37. *Kena Upaniṣad* (2.1)

yadi manyase suvedeti daharam evāpi nūnaṃ tvaṃ vettha brahmaṇo rūpam
yad asya tvaṃ yad asya deveṣv atha nu mīmāṃsyam eva te manye viditam.

If you think, "I know it well," then you know just a little about the nature (form) of Brahman, that part of it which is yourself and that part of it which exists amongst the gods. I think, therefore, that you should consider more deeply that which you seek to know.

This verse from the *Kena Upanishad* is all about knowledge of higher truths, and cites the words of a teacher spoken to a slightly presumptuous student. The student is a scholar of the Vedas, and has probably studied the sacred texts for many years. Hence he 'knows' the Vedas, and seems to think that he can apply the same method of knowing to the subject of Brahman, the highest spiritual reality. The point being made is that the 'knowing' of Brahman is different from knowledge of other subjects, which is gained through research and study. Knowledge of Brahman is about a change in consciousness, and the awakening of higher realization, which requires more than mundane learning.

ESSENCE SEEKERS

38. *Chāndogya Upaniṣad* (6.9.1)

1. *yathā somya, madhu madhukṛto nistiṣthanti, nānātyayānāṃ vṛkṣāṇāṃ rasān samanvahāram ekatāṃ rasaṃ gamayanti.*

2. *te yathā tatra na vivekaṃ labhante 'muṣyāhaṃ vṛkṣasya raso'smi, amuṣyāhaṃ vṛkṣasya raso 'smy amuṣyāhaṃ vṛkṣasya raso 'smīty evam eva khalu saumyemāh sarvāh prajāh sati sampadya na viduḥ sati sampadyāmaha iti.*

1. My dear son, it is just like the bees who prepare honey by collecting the nectar from different trees and reducing them into one essence.

2. These juices do not discriminate saying, 'I am the juice of that tree, and I am the nectar of that tree'. Similarly, my dear son, when all these different creatures reach the existent, they do not know they have reached that state.

The *Chandogya* is one of the oldest and most important of the *Upanishads*, and it is here that we find clear expressions of the philosophy of *Advaita*, the doctrine of absolute unity. For most of the *Upanishads,* and for Shankaracharya, there is one absolute reality, and the variety and individuality we observe is a lesser reality. The aim is to transcend the lesser reality and achieve the state of absolute reality, which is Brahman alone. Here the *Upanishad* uses the example of bees making honey. They draw nectar from different types of flowers, but the ultimate reality they create is honey, without there being differentiation between the types of flower nectar it contains. In the same way, we observe different creatures and different people, but the higher reality we must realize is that all are the same Brahman, the one absolute existence.

LIKE RIVERS TO THE SEA

39. *Chāndogya Upaniṣad* (6.10.1-3)

1. *imāḥ somya nadyaḥ purastāt prācyaḥ syandante paścāt pratīcyas tāḥ samudrāt samudram evāpiyanti sa samudra eva bhavati tā yathā tatra na vidur iyam aham asmīti.*

2. *evam eva khalu, somyemāḥ sarvāḥ prajāḥ sata āgamya na viduḥ, sata āgamya na viduḥ sata āgacchāmaha iti ta iha vyāghro vā siṃho vā vṛko vā varāho vā kīṭo vā pataṅgo vā dāṃśo vā maśako vā yad yad bhavanti tad ābhavanti.*

3. *sa ya eṣo'ṇimaitad ātmyam idaṃ sarvaṃ tat satyaṃ sa ātmā tat tvam asi śvetaketo iti*

1. See these rivers, my dear son, the easterly flow towards the east, the westerly flow towards the west. From the sea they become the sea again; they become the sea alone. When this occurs, these rivers do not know 'I am this one, I am that one.'

2. Similarly, my dear son, all these living beings, when they reach the true reality do not know, 'Now we are reaching the true reality.' Whatever they are in this

world, tiger or lion or wolf or boar or worm or fly or gnat or mosquito, they all merge into that reality.

3. That which is the subtle essence, that is the self of this whole world, that is truth, that is the *atman*. That is what you are, Svetaketu.

This is one of the most famous passages from the *Upanishads*, not least because it concludes with the phrase '*tat tvam asi*', meaning, 'you are that', or, 'that is what you are'. The example used here is that of rivers, which have an individual identity as they flow across the land, but all become the same ocean when they reach the sea. Similarly, the *atman* present as the soul of all beings is nothing but Brahman, and the variety we perceive in individual living entities is no more than a lesser reality. The absolute reality is Brahman alone, and according to the *Upanishad* that is our true identity; that is what we are.

COMPLETENESS

40. *Iśa Upaniṣad* (Invocation)

oṃ pūrṇam adaḥ pūrṇam idaṃ pūrṇāt pūrṇam udacyate
pūrṇasya pūrṇam ādāya pūrṇam evāvaśiṣyate.

Om. That is complete; this is complete. The complete has come into being from out of the complete. After the complete has emerged from the complete, the original complete remains as it was.

Although this *Upanishad* is titled *Isa*, which means Lord, the philosophy is parallel to that of the other major *Upanishads*. There is an absolute reality from which all things come and to which all things must return. This invocation is recited during Hindu ceremonies and is often chanted during funerals. It can serve as a reminder that the fullness of Brahman remains undiminished and eternal, and no matter what difficulties or sufferings may exist, the material level of existence is only temporary, whilst the absolute reality of the divine is always complete. Even though the created world comes from Brahman, the absolute Brahman is not diminished thereby. This is logically inconceivable, but of course, Brahman is not subject to the powers of human reason.

IT'S ALL IN THE HEART

41. *Chāndogya Upaniṣad* (8.1.3)

sa brūyāt: yāvān vā ayam ākāśas tāvān eso'ntarhṛdaya ākāśa ubhe asmin dyāvā-pṛthivī antar eva samāhite ubhāv agniś ca vāyuś ca sūryā-candramasāv ubhau vidyun nakṣatrāṇi yac cāsyehāsti yac ca nāsti sarvaṃ tad asmin samāhitam iti.

He should say, "As far as space extends, this is how far the space within one's heart extends. Within it, indeed are both heaven and earth, both fire and air, both the sun and the moon, lightning and stars. Whatever there is in this world, and whatever there is not, all of this is contained within it.

This verse from the *Chandogya Upanishad* presents a very uplifting concept. The modern worldview is one of insufficiency, that we are not enough, which can often leave people feeling inadequate. The *Upanishad* teaches us that there is an infinite reality within our hearts, which encompasses all that exists and all that does not exist. It is within this heart space that liberation is found, and nowhere else. It is awe inspiring to read verses such as this one, through which the great *Upanishad*s leave us with the feeling that there is a greatness beyond, which we can conceive of as hidden right here within each and every one of us. Brahman is the one absolute reality, and because the *atman* is identical with Brahman, everything that exists is contained within the *atman*, within one's own being.

BRAHMAN OFFERING TO BRAHMAN

42. *The Bhagavad Gītā* (4.24)

24. *brahmārpaṇaṃ brahma-havir brahmāgnau brahmaṇā hutam*
brahmaiva tena gantavyaṃ brahma-karma-samādhinā

24. The sacrificial offering is Brahman. The oblation is Brahman; Brahman offers it into the fire that is also Brahman. Brahman alone is reached by a person who absorbs his mind completely in the ritual act that is Brahman.

This verse from the *Bhagavad Gita* can be interpreted metaphysically; it describes the Vedic ritual according to the philosophy of the *Upanishads.* Krishna teaches us that all the different aspects of the offering are nothing but Brahman. When seen in this way, any ritual enactment can be performed with this higher understanding. This verse can form the basis for all of our actions. It is often recited before a meal, so that it is understood that the act of eating is Brahman, the food is Brahman, the individual eating is Brahman, and the fire of digestion is Brahman. In this way, every act, even the simple act of eating, is transformed into an act of absorbing oneself more completely into an elevated state of consciousness. One may feel that one who is seeking realization of Brahman should give up all forms of religious ritual. Krishna, however, has a different opinion. The ritual life must be continued, partly as an example to others, and partly because the ritual itself becomes a part of the spiritual quest when it is performed with consciousness of Brahman.

BRAHMAN

43. *Māṇḍūkya Upaniṣad* (2)

2. *sarvaṃ hy etad brahmāyam ātmā brahma so 'yam ātmā catuṣpāt*

2. This whole world is Brahman; this *ātman* is Brahman; this same *ātman* exists in four ways.

The statements made in this passage from the *Mandukya Upanishad* are expressed in a simple and succinct form, but they express the most profound spiritual truths. To understand the third of these, that the *atman* exists in four ways, one has to read the complete *Upanishad*, but the other two statements express ideas that have had an enduring influence over Indian religious thought. The first statement, *sarvam hy etad brahma*, indicates that the identity of all reality is Brahman alone, regardless of the external appearance we perceive moment by moment. The second, *ayam atma brahma*, asserts in a straightforward manner that the soul is Brahman, thereby expressing the identity of every being with God, the ultimate reality. This aphorism was selected by Shankaracharya as one of his *Mahavakya*, or great sayings, of the *Upanishads*, and one can readily perceive how it confirms the fundamental precept of his philosophy of absolute oneness.

SELF-REALISATION

44. *Kaṭha Upaniṣad* (6.12-13)

12. *naiva vācā na manasā prāptuṃ śakyo na cakṣuṣā*
astīti bruvato 'nyatra kathaṃ tad upalabhyate

13. *astīty evopalabdhavyas tattva-bhāvena cobhayoḥ*
astīty evopalabdhasya tattva-bhāvaḥ prasīdati

12. The *ātman* cannot be realized by words, or by thoughts, and neither can the eye perceive it. How can it be realized by anyone other than one who simply says, 'It is'?

13. There are only two ways in which the *ātman* can be grasped, one is by asserting 'It is', and the other is by knowing it is real. When one has the realization 'It is', then the knowledge that it is real becomes clear.

If the *atman* is beyond the capacity of the mind and senses, then how can we know for sure that it exists, let alone achieve realization? The *Katha Upanishad* seems to provide a very logical and straightforward teaching about how we can understand the higher self. First, we can simply declare that it exists; many followers of the devotional path will never question the exact nature of the divine, but rather declare that God exists and continue to reap the benefits of fulfilling worship. Although this is a fruitful understanding, the enlightened being who has actually had the internal realization of the *atman* will fully comprehend the highest truth. The *atman* is beyond the range of mind, words, or senses, and so must be realized by a higher form of perception. In this way, the *Katha Upanishad* introduces us to the idea of yoga meditation, as taught by Patañjali and by Krishna in the *Bhagavad Gita*. The control of the mind allows one to develop an alternative mode of perception, which leads in turn to realization of the absolute nature of the *atman* within all beings.

I AM BRAHMAN

45. *Bṛhad Āraṇyaka Upaniṣad* (1.4.10)

10. *tad dhaitat paśyann ṛṣir vāmadevaḥ pratipede ahaṃ manur abhavam sūryaś ceti*
tad idam apy etarhi ya evaṃ veda ahaṃ brahmāsmīti sa idaṃ sarvaṃ bhavati

10. On realizing this truth, the Rishi Vāmadeva concluded, "I was Manu and I was the sun." Even now, anyone who reaches this same understanding of "I am Brahman," becomes this whole world.

The *Brihad Aranyaka Upanishad* is often considered by scholars to be the oldest of the *Upanishads*. In this verse, we hear the words of the great Rishi Vamadeva who upon becoming enlightened, in this higher state, goes beyond his material condition of identifying with his body and mind, and sees himself as all things, including the sun. He then states '*aham brahmasmi*', 'I am Brahman,' which is one of the 'great sayings' (*Mahavakyas*) of Advaita philosophy. The enlightened state whereby we identify with all things is achieved with the realization of oneness with Brahman. Whilst in the consciousness of this world, Vamadeva had thought of himself as an individual person, but now his consciousness and his identity have changed. Now he is one with the entire world, now he is one with Brahman.

AWAKENED KNOWING

46. *Kena Upaniṣad* (2.4)

pratibodha-viditam matam amṛtatvaṃ hi vindate
ātmanā vindate vīryam vidyayā vindate amṛtam.

It is known when understood through realization (awakening); then one gains the state of immortality. One gains power through one's self (*ātman*); one gains immortality through knowing.

The *Kena Upanishad* is primarily concerned with disseminating the idea that we cannot 'know' Brahman through conventional means of knowing. Rather it uses the wonderful term *pratibodha viditam,* 'awakened knowing', to describe a higher state of knowing. If the light is switched off in a room, we may still be able to feel objects, and understand what they are individually, but once the light is turned on, then we can have true realization. Not only is this an awakened state whereby liberation is achieved, but a state by which all other aspects of our awareness also become enlightened. Learning spiritual truths by conventional means, such as studying the *Upanishads,* can only take us so far. For full realization of Brahman, a different means of knowing is required, and it is this higher means of knowing that the *Kena Upanishad* is referring to here.

LIKE A SPIDER'S WEB

47. *Muṇḍaka Upaniṣad* (1.1.7)

yathorṇa-nābhiḥ srjate gṛhṇate ca yathā pṛthivyām oṣadhayaḥ sambhavanti
yathā sataḥ puruṣāt keśalomāni tathākṣarāt sambhavatīha viśvam.

Just as a spider sends forth its web and draws it back in, just as plants grow from the earth, as hair grows on a living being's head and body, so from the imperishable the whole universe arises.

The *Upanishads* are full of excellent analogies, which seek to convey to us the doctrine of oneness with Brahman. These examples are designed to show that we are constantly connected to our spiritual source. With this knowledge, one can never feel alone, for we are all part of the divine reality. Just as apples are on a tree, all things are part of Brahman. The spiders' web, the hair on our body, and the plants growing from the earth all appear to have an individual identity, but ultimately they are one with their source. In the same way, we all regard ourselves as individual, distinctive living beings, but the higher realization, as presented by the *Upanishads*, comprehends the unity of this entire existence.

DESIRE

48. *Harivaṃśa* (1.30.44)

yac ca kāma-sukhaṃ loke yac ca divyaṃ mahat sukham
tṛṣṇā-kṣaya-sukhasyaite nārhataḥ ṣodaśīṃ kalām.

The pleasures of this world when desires are fulfilled, and the greater joys of heaven, are not equal to a sixteenth part of the satisfaction that comes from the cessation of hankering for such pleasure.

The *Harivamsa* is considered as a supplementary book to the *Mahabharata*, and contains a detailed account of Krishna's life. The teaching in this verse is highly relevant in relation to the modern, desire-led mentality. Although there may be many objects of desire in the world, many things we want to achieve and places we want to go, we often find that the joy experienced once we have consumed our objects of desire leaves us unsatisfied. Even if we fulfil every desire in the world, and even if we experience the pleasures of heaven, we will not achieve even a tiny amount of satisfaction when compared to living a life free from constant hankering. It is not a life of empty pleasures but a life lived helping others, a life based on Sanatana Dharma, which is the source of real joyfulness.

GOD IN ALL BEINGS

49. *Bhāgavata Purāṇa* (3.29.22)

yo mām sarveṣu bhūteṣu santam ātmānam īśvaraṃ
īśvaraṃ hitvārcāṃ bhajate mauḍhyād bhasmany eva juhoti saḥ

If a person disregards me as the lord who is the *ātman* present within all beings and due to ignorance chooses merely to worship me as the lord, then his offerings simply turn to ashes.

The *Bhagavata Purana* is a very significant work dedicated to Vishnu, mostly in the form of Krishna. Here Krishna says, "I am the lord and the soul of all living beings, we should not blindly disregard the lord who exists within others." One can imagine devotees who enter temples with extravagant offerings, but turn a blind eye to the desperately needy sitting outside the walls of the temple. It is this disregard that we can be inspired to transcend. Feeding the poor is worshipping God, for God exists as the soul of all beings, and this is something we cannot neglect. The *Bhagavad Gita* speaks of there being two paths, one based on realized knowledge and the other devotion to God. Here the point is made that one must be aware of both forms of practice, and not adhere to only one, whilst condemning the other. One may be inclined towards acts of devotion and developing a mood of loving surrender, but that does not mean that one should condemn or criticize those who are more inclined towards the path of knowledge.

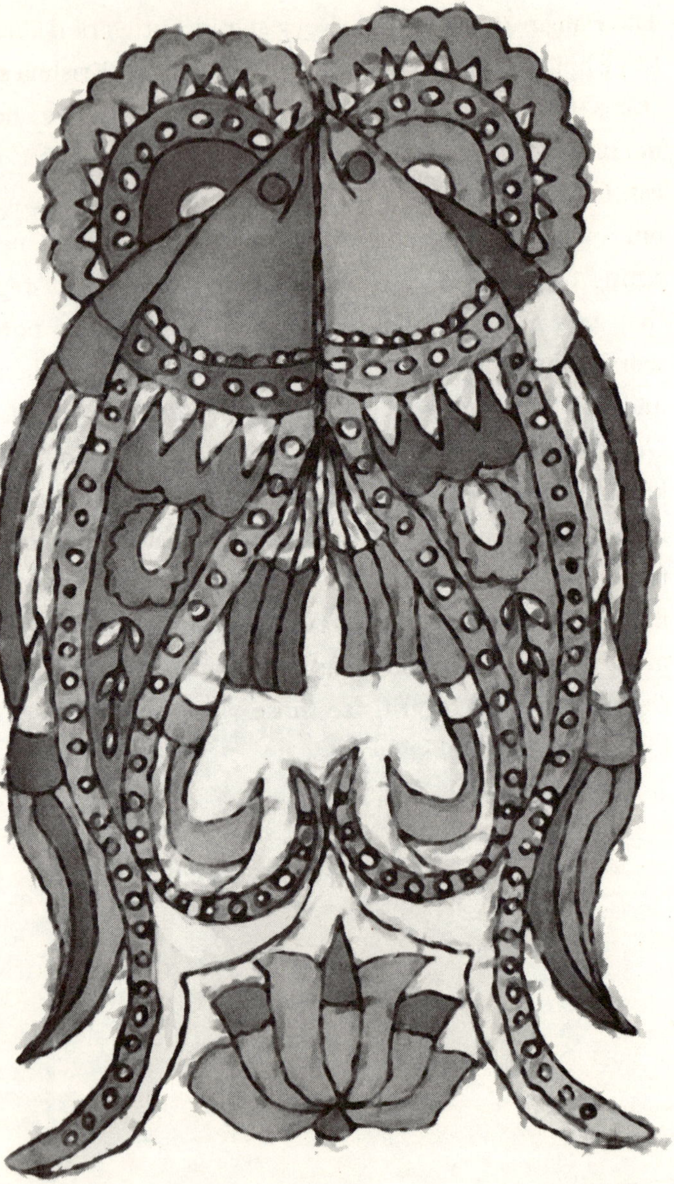

BIRDS ON A TREE

50. *Muṇḍaka Upaniṣad* (3.1-2)

1. *dvā suparṇā sayujā sakhāyā samānaṃ vṛkṣam pariṣasvajāte tayor*
   tayor anyaḥ pippalaṃ svādv atty anaśnan anyo'bhicākaśīti.

2. *samāne vṛkṣe puruṣo nimagno'nīśayā śocati muhyamānaḥ juṣṭam yadā paśyaty anyam īśam asya mahimānam iti, vīta-śokaḥ.*

1. Two birds who are friends always sit together on the same tree. One of the two eats the sweet fruit, whilst the other watches without eating.

2. Situated on that same tree, one being is grieving; deluded by she who is not the Lord. But when he sees the other, who is the Lord, and his greatness, he becomes free from suffering.

Each of us has two birds within us, one is constantly hankering, wishing to fulfil his or her desires, but the other is the witness, the Lord, who resides within all of us. Most of us are pulled in the direction of the objects of our desires, experiencing both happiness and sadness, but without any lasting happiness. The only way to achieve freedom from this suffering is to turn inwards towards the Lord, and see that the fluctuations of the world are nothing but transitory ebbs and flows within the absolute reality. Some commentators take the two birds to be the *atman* in its liberated and non-liberated states, but those inclined towards a theistic understanding suggest that there is a manifestation of God within each of us, guiding us through the cycle of death and rebirth. It is up to each individual to decide which reading is the more valid. 'She who is not the lord' almost certainly means the world of matter, which deludes the living being and keeps it in a state of bondage.

DEVOTION AND KNOWLEDGE

51. *Śiva Purāṇa* (*Rudra Samhitā*, *Satī Khaṇḍa*, 23.16-17)

16. *bhaktau jñāne na bhedo hi tat kartuḥ sarvadā sukham*
vijñānaṃ na bhavaty eva sati bhakti-virodhinaḥ

17. *bhaktyādhīnaḥ sadāhaṃ vai tat-prabhāvād gṛheṣv api*
nīcānāṃ jāti-hīnānāṃ yāmi devi na saṃśayaḥ

16. There is no distinction between devotion and realized knowledge, and one who engages in acts of devotion will experience constant joy. Realized knowledge is never attained, O Satī, by one who rejects devotion.

17. I am always rendered subservient by devotion, and on the strength of their devotion, I go to the houses of persons of the lower castes or of those outside the caste system. There can be no doubting this, O Goddess.

Whilst in conversation with the Goddess Parvati, Lord Shiva explains in the *Shiva Purana* that the true path to enlightenment is the *bhakti marga*, the path of loving devotion. In many of the world's religious traditions, the method of relating to the divine is through reverence and worship. Here Lord Shiva explains something very interesting; not only is he pleased by the love of his devotees, but he is rendered subservient to them. This is a teaching on the power of bhakti, and there are many wonderful examples in Hindu scriptures of devotees, who out of pure love of God overcome life's arduous circumstances through divine assistance. In an earlier verse from the *Bhagavata*, the point was made that those who follow the way of devotion should never disregard the need for realized knowledge. Here the point is made from the opposite perspective, as Lord Shiva declares that devotion is essential even for those on the path of knowledge; both forms of spirituality are required, and are in fact a part of the same path of spiritual progression.

THE NATURE OF GOD

52. *Śiva Purāṇa* (*Rudra Saṃhitā*, *Sṛṣṭi Khaṇḍa*, 9.27)

27. *śrī maheśa uvāca*
pralaya-sthiti-sargāṇāṃ kartāhaṃ sa-guṇo 'guṇaḥ
para-brahma nirvikārī sac-cid-ānanda-lakṣaṇaḥ

27. Srī Maheśa said: Being without attributes, I assume attributes and perform the work of destruction, maintenance, and creation of the world. I am the Supreme Brahman, unchanging, defined only by the qualities of existence, consciousness, and bliss (*sat, chit,* and *ānanda*).

What is the nature of God? Is God with or without attributes? We learn from the *Shiva Purana*, which is one of the *Mahapuranas*, that the lord assumes a form to allow the world to exist. In this verse, we see that Lord Shiva is the supreme Brahman, which is beyond all forms, beyond the cycle of creation, maintenance, and destruction of the world, and even beyond all understanding. Lord Shiva is described here by the popular term Satchitananda; he is the ultimate divine principle. Many people find it difficult to believe in an anthropomorphic Deity, as is described in many of the world's scriptures, but here we learn that all such forms are merely those assumed by God for his purposes in this world. The ultimate nature of God is beyond all such designations, and is beyond all power of description.

THE ETERNAL ELEMENT

53. *The Bhagavad Gītā* (15.7)

7. *mamaivāṃśo jīva-loke jīva-bhūtaḥ sanātanaḥ*
manaḥ-ṣaṣṭhānīndriyāṇi prakṛti-sthāni karṣati

7. The eternal living element, existing in this world of living beings, is nothing but a part of me. It draws to itself the five senses and the mind, which is the sixth, all of which reside in *prakṛti* (matter).

Chapter fifteen of the *Bhagavad Gita* is often termed the yoga of the supreme self. Krishna here explains that the eternal soul, which resides within the world and in all beings, is none other than himself. The words used are *prakriti sthani*, which literally mean standing within matter. Krishna tells us that our mind and our five senses are of the material world, and incapable of illuminating the nature of the divine, which permeates all things. Once one has transcended the mind and the five senses, the goal of life has been achieved and liberation from rebirth obtained. The relationship between the *atman* and Krishna is here described as being that between the part and the whole. Some commentators will insist that the part is nothing but the whole, just as the wave is the nothing but the ocean. But others assert that the part is one with and yet distinct from the whole. Again, it is up to the reader to decide which interpretation is more suitable.

ONE TRUTH, MANY NAMES

54. *Rigveda Saṃhitā* (1.164.46)

46. *indraṃ mitraṃ varuṇam agnim āhur atho divyaḥ sa suparṇo garutmān*
ekaṃ sad viprā bahudhā vadanty agniṃ yamaṃ mātariśvānam āhuḥ

46. They speak of Indra, Mitra, Varuna, and Agni, or else of the celestial bird Garutmān. There is but one reality here, though the seers refer to it in many different ways; hence they speak of Agni, Yama or Mātariśvān.

This is one of the most famous verses of the *Rigveda Samhita.* In many ways, it is a foundational assertion for Hinduism as a religion today. Many Hindus memorize this verse, and it is often quoted as a high-minded ideal for interfaith dialogue. Although we may approach the divine in different forms, we must realize that underpinning all things there is one supreme reality. Hinduism has this unique quality of being able to incorporate seemingly conflicting ideas into its spiritually pluralistic outlook. This verse teaches us why Hindus often find it very easy to celebrate the festivals of other religions, and even to worship with followers of other traditions. Internally also, the majority of Hindus will see no conflict in worshipping Shiva at one moment and Vishnu the next. It is this idea which has permeated Hindu thought for thousands of years, the truth is one, and the wise will call it by many names, *ekam sad vipra bahudha vadanti.*

ONE FIRE, MANY FLAMES

55. *Rig Veda* (8.58.2)

eka evāgnir bahudhā samiddhaekaḥ sūryo viśvam anu prabhūtaḥekaivoṣāh sarvam idaṃ vibhāty ekaṃ vā idaṃ vibabhūva sarvam.

The one fire burns in many ways; the one sun illuminates the entire world when it rises; this one dawn dispels the darkness throughout the entire world. This one alone is present in all things.

Here is another verse from one of the world's oldest religious texts, the *Rigveda Samhita*, teaching about the one true reality present within the world. The teaching behind these analogies is that when we see the one within all things, then all darkness is dispelled. In the *Upanishads*, the one is called Brahman, but here it is made clear that the name is not important. What is required is the understanding that there is one true reality underpinning everything, and with the realisation of that truth, all darkness is removed.

SHIVA AND VISHNU

56. *The Mahābhārata* (12.328.23-24)

23. *pramāṇāni hi pūjyāni tatas taṃ pūjayāmy aham*
yas taṃ vetti sa māṃ vetti yo 'nu taṃ sa hi māṃ anu

24. *rudro nārāyaṇaś caiva sattvaṃ ekaṃ dvidhā-kṛtam*
loke carati kaunteya vyakti-sthaṃ sarva-karmasu

23. These rules must be respected, and for this reason, I offer my worship to him. One who knows him knows myself, and one who knows myself knows him as well.

24. Rudra and Nārāyaṇa are but one being, manifest in two different ways, manifest in the world, and present in all actions performed.

This verse further emphasises one of the great strengths of Sanatana Dharma as an ideal model of religion, its pluralistic outlook. Arjuna asks Krishna why he would worship Shiva, and the response by Krishna is that he does so to set an example for the world. However, for the one who truly knows, Shiva and Krishna are not different. Religion in the past has been responsible for terrible wrongdoing. When people are led to believe that salvation is only found through their own tradition, the outcome is often a justification for the inflicting of suffering and persecution on the non-believers. Here Krishna says that it is the same God who is worshipped in different ways. This understanding not only sets an ideal of mutual respect, but one of accepting the spiritual path of another as being just as valid as one's own. In India, there are Vaishnavas and Shaivites, but the vast majority of Hindus worship the Deity in both these forms, instinctively recognising the truth revealed in these two verses.

I AM THE ATMAN

57. *The Bhagavad Gītā* (10.20)

20. *aham ātmā guḍākeśa sarva-bhūtāśaya-sthitaḥ*
aham ādiś ca madhyaṃ bhūtānām anta eva ca

20. I am the *ātman*, Gudākeśa, situated in the heart of all beings. I am the beginning and the middle of living beings, and their end as well.

Here Krishna states that he is the *atman*, the divine reality that resides in the heart of all beings. By the word heart, we can safely say it is not the physical heart being referred to, but the true self, which is of a pure spiritual nature. The important point here is the identity between the *atman* and God, which is such a prominent feature of Hindu theology. The Supreme Deity exists in his own abode, but he is also present within each being, and all of us are not just creations but are a part of the divine. Through spiritual practice, or divine grace, it becomes possible to rediscover that pure spiritual identity. The second part of the verse states that Krishna is the beginning, middle, and end of all living beings, indicating that our existence is dependent on God and that we are a part of his divine nature.

LIKE JEWELS ON A THREAD

58. *The Bhagavad Gītā* (7.7)

7. *mattaḥ parataraṃ nānyat kiṃcid asti dhanaṃjaya*
mayi sarvaṃ idaṃ protaṃ sūtre maṇi-gaṇā iva

7. There is no other thing superior to me, Dhanaṃjaya. This whole world rests upon me, just as jewels are strung upon a thread.

There is nothing higher than God, or Brahman. All realities and levels of consciousness are lower states of existence. The first line of this verse is a classic statement of Indian monotheism, as Krishna clearly asserts he is the one beyond whom there is no other. In the analogy used here, Krishna is the hidden thread under the necklace of jewels. We can imagine a necklace which is held together in this way; if the thread were removed, the jewels would fall apart and drop into chaos, crashing in all directions. The sense of order, the sense of things being held together, is only due to the spiritual underpinning. The world is a wonderful place, and at times, we may wonder how it is that such an ordered system of existence came to be. Here it is revealed that there is an unseen reality, which holds the ordered system in place. This omnipresent reality is Krishna himself. This analogy is a wonderful way of understanding and relating to God as we attempt to gain realisation of his unseen presence in this world.

THE ORIGIN

59. *The Bhagavad Gītā* (10.8)

8. *ahaṃ sarvasya prabhavo mattaḥ sarvaṃ pravartate*
iti matvā bhajante māṃ budhā bhāva-samanvitāḥ

8. I am the origin of all things; everything comes into being from out of me. Understanding this, the enlightened ones worship me, filled with loving attachment.

This is another famous verse from the *Bhagavad Gita.* Krishna explains that he is the spiritual source of all things. The whole world comes into being from this single source, just as a tree with all its branches and leaves appears from a single seed. The ones who have this enlightened realisation engage in loving devotion towards Krishna. The word used is *bhajante,* which literally means to engage in acts of love and worship. The idea here is that spiritual realisation must lead to various forms of spiritual practice. In other words, realisation is not just a state of consciousness, but will always be reflected in the way one lives one's life. Realization of Krishna's divine supremacy naturally impels the enlightened person towards acts of worship and a mood of loving devotion.

NON-COVETING

60. *Iśa Upaniṣad* (1)

īśāvāsyam idaṃ sarvaṃ yat kiṃca jagatyāṃ jagat
tena tyaktena bhuñjīthā mā gṛdhaḥ kasyasvid dhanam

All this is to be pervaded by the Lord, whatever there is that moves and changes within this world of transformation. One should thus live on what others have abandoned, and never covet the wealth of any other person.

The word Isha means Lord or ruler, but the philosophy of the *Isha Upanishad* describes the Lord as the all-pervading spiritual existence that is Brahman. One of Hinduism's great modern teachers, Mahatma Gandhi, said, "If all the *Upanishads* and all the other scriptures happened suddenly to be reduced to ashes, and if only the first verse in the *Ishopanishad* were left in the memory of the Hindus, Hinduism would live for ever". It is in this verse that we are taught that God, or the universal divine presence, pervades all that exists, and based on that understanding we should always be content, regardless of what we do or do not possess. If we have the realisation that the divine pervades all things, then we will never hanker after the belongings of others, and we can peacefully coexist with each other. Gandhiji felt that this spiritual perspective of the *Isha Upanishad* was the essence of Hindu thought, and the solution for many of the world's problems. Again, we see how realisation of the higher truth is not simply a process of the mind, but is reflected in the way we live in the world, and the ways in which we interact with other living beings.

ONLY LOVE

61. *The Bhagavad Gītā* (18.66)

66. *sarva-dharmān parityajya mām ekaṃ śaraṇaṃ vraja*
ahaṃ tvā sarva-pāpebhyo mokṣayiṣyāmi mā śucaḥ

66. Abandoning all types of dharma, find shelter with me alone. I will deliver you from all sins; do not grieve.

In one of the concluding verses of the *Bhagavad Gita*, Krishna urges Arjuna towards the state of *sharanam*, surrendering everything unto him. The act of surrendering is a subtle one; often we feel as if there is a higher calling in life, and if we surrender our ego, desires, goals, duties, and everything, unto God, then every action becomes a divine offering. Our life becomes an offering; this again is a part of the process of Bhakti Yoga. We may feel that although we aspire towards the path of dharma, and seek spiritual goals, this is very difficult to achieve. Here Krishna reassures his devoted cousin that if one becomes entirely dependent upon him, then he will overcome all obstacles on behalf of the surrendered person. The spiritual perfection of liberation from rebirth may seem impossible to achieve, but for Krishna everything is possible. Like a loving father, he will take care of all the difficulties we face; all that is required is *sharanam*, complete dependence.

WHOM KRISHNA LOVES

62. *The Bhagavad Gītā* (12.13-14)

12. *adveṣṭā sarva-bhūtānāṃ maitraḥ karuṇa eva ca*
nirmamo nirahaṃkāraḥ sama-duḥkha-sukhaḥ kṣamī

13. *santuṣṭaḥ satataṃ yogī yatātmā dṛḍha-niścayaḥ*
mayy arpita-mano-buddhir yo mad-bhaktaḥ sa me priyaḥ

12. He has no hatred for any living being, he shows goodwill and compassion; he has no sense of ownership, and no pride; he remains equal in misery and joy, and he has the quality of endurance;

13. He is always contented, he is a *yogin* who possesses self-control; he is firm in his commitment, and he absorbs his mind and intellect in me; such a devotee is loved by me.

Krishna here describes the type of devotee that he loves. The first point is that before the characteristics of devotion are detailed, Krishna describes the qualities of Sanatana Dharma, which we have observed earlier in this book. He also explains that this is an individual who is in the world but not of it. He is one whose consciousness is absorbed in Krishna, and as a result is not swayed by the changing conditions of the world. This is the mentality sought by the *bhakti-yogin*. Also of great significance here is the final phrase, *yo mad-bhaktah sa me priyah*, as this indicates that despite his all-pervasive identity as the soul of every being, the deity still enters into a relationship of reciprocated love with those who dedicate themselves to him. In the previous verse we considered, Krishna said that he would deliver one who surrendered to him from all problems, and here he explains why he does this; it is because of the relationship of mutual love that exists between himself and the devotee.

THE LOVE OF THE GOPIS

63. *Bhāgavata Purāṇa* (10.31.2)

2. *śarad-udāśaye sādhu-jāta-sat-sarasijodara-śrī-muṣā dṛśā surata-nātha te 'śulka-dāsikā varada nighnato neha kiṃ vadhaḥ*

2. Your looks of love are more pleasing than the opulence found in the heart of a lotus flower, grown to its full beauty on a lake in the autumn season. O lord of lovemaking, O granter of boons, we are your maidservants who seek no payment for our service. Do not destroy us here. How can you afflict us in this way?

The loving devotion of the *gopis* for Krishna is considered by many to be the highest example of spiritual love, of *bhakti*. The process of *bhakti* is to transform oneself into a vessel for loving God, so that one's every act becomes an offering to God, and every thought is wasted unless it be focussed on the beloved lord. Rather than the austere form of meditation prescribed in texts such as Patanjali's *Yoga Sutras*, this form of yoga is full of sweetness, as the devotee surrenders to the grace of the Lord. In this way, the spiritual aspirant becomes an embodiment of love and devotion. These wonderful narratives of the *gopis* with Krishna are found in Book Ten of the *Bhagavata Purana*, which is full of beautiful stories describing the outpouring of love exhibited by Krishna's devotees. It is said that once he has tasted this love, no amount of worldly pleasure can satisfy a person.

THE MOOD OF DEVOTION

64. *Bhāgavata Purāṇa* (10.31.10)

10. *prahasitaṃ priya-prema-vīkṣaṇaṃ viharaṇaṃ ca te dhyāna-maṅgalam*
rahasi saṃvido yā hṛdi spṛśaḥ kuhaka no manaḥ kṣobhayanti hi

10. Your smile, your affectionate loving glances, and your playful activities, are delightful objects of meditation. The private conversations we had with you in solitary places similarly touch the heart. It is these thoughts, O deceiver, that disturb our minds.

This verse is again from the tenth book of the *Bhagavata Purana*. Through his divine grace, Krishna has cast his loving glance upon the *gopis*. They become so overwhelmed with love that nothing else compares. This form of spirituality has shaped the way Hindus worship God in the modern world. To have the *darshan* of Krishna, to read about his playful activities, to meditate upon his name, and to dance before his image, are all means through which to cultivate the mood of loving devotion sought through *bhakti*. The language of *bhakti* is the language of love; this is not an intellectual pursuit but an affair of the heart. At one point, these young women affectionately address the Lord as *kuhaka*, the deceiver, thereby revealing the intimacy of their love, which is far removed from the sense of awe typically associated with devotion to God. In Vrindaban, love alone prevails.

CONTROLLING THE MIND

65. *The Bhagavad Gītā* (6.25)

25. *śanaiḥ śanair uparamed buddhyā dhṛti-gṛhītayā*
ātma-saṃsthaṃ manaḥ kṛtvā na kiṃcid api cintayet

25. One should undertake this withdrawal of the mind little by little, using the resolutely focused intellect. Absorbing the mind entirely in the *ātman*, one should not think of any other object.

To strengthen a muscle, exercise must be undertaken and little-by- little, physical strength is achieved. Krishna advises that exactly the same method be applied to the mind, so that over time, and with consistent effort, the intellect can come to focus on the *atman* alone. The sensory world of desires pulls us in every direction, but if with dedication, we can engage ourselves in the practice of yoga, we can then develop the ability to turn our vision inward. The *Upanishads* speak of realised knowledge as being the means by which liberation from this world is attained, and the early yoga teachings offer a systematic technique by means of which such knowledge can be gained. First, the mind must be brought under control. Then it can be used as a tool of inward exploration through meditation on the inner self. Eventually, the adept in yoga comes to perceive the *atman* directly, and the knowledge revealed by the *Upanishads* then becomes the realized knowledge required for full spiritual enlightenment.

YOGA AND ACTION

66. *The Bhagavad Gītā* (2.50)

50. buddhi-yukto jahātīha ubhe sukṛta-duṣkṛte
tasmād yogāya yujyasva yogaḥ karmasu kauśalam

50. Focusing the intellect in this way, one transcends both righteous and unrighteous deeds. Therefore, engage yourself in this Yoga, for Yoga is in fact the art of performing action.

When we act in the world, we produce karma, which can be good or bad. Here Krishna states that it is entirely possible to transcend both the good and bad karmic consequences that arise from our actions. The equilibrium achieved by a karma *yogin* is not attained by working to fulfil selfish desires, but from a sense of high-minded selfless duty in performing one's work. Abandoning the desire for personal gain, and all fear of failure, one can continue to work in the world without acquiring karmic reactions. Krishna says that this method of working in the world represents a higher state of existence, a state in which we become free from the bondage of karma and rebirth, a state that leads to liberation. The word 'Yoga' here does not indicate the meditational practices mentioned previously, but rather a way of living in the world without attachment. This 'art of performing action' is referred to as a Karma Yoga in the *Bhagavad Gita.*

WHAT IS YOGA?

67. *Patañjali Yoga Sūtras* (1.1-4)

1. *atha yogānuśāsanam*
2. *yogaś citta-vṛtti-nirodhaḥ*
3. *tadā draṣṭuḥ sva-rūpe 'vasthānam*
4. *vṛtti-sārūpyam itaratra*

1. Here is the teaching on Yoga.
2. Yoga is the restriction of the movements of the mind.
3. When this is achieved, the witness comes to exist in terms of its own identity.
4. Otherwise, the witness assumes the identity dictated by the movements of the mind.

Patanjali's *Yoga Sutras* is unique among the foundational treatises of Hinduism's *darshanas* or philosophical systems. Rather than trying to explain the nature of the world, it is primarily concerned with the practices we should adopt to transcend the world. It is in these four initial *sutras* that Patanjali defines yoga. He states that yoga is simply the stilling of mental fluctuations. It is this state of stillness, which allows one to live in terms of one's true *svarupa* (identity), which is as the *atman* rather than as the body and the mind. However, if we do not achieve this control, we are allowing ourselves to be pulled by the *vrittis* (the movements of the mind). Not only will these uncontrolled movements define how we act, but they will also define who we are. We will then exist in relation to this world, and remain unaware of our true spiritual identity. When the *vrittis* are stilled, the inner spirit shines forth like a lamp that is free of all contamination.

YOGA POSTURE

68. *The Bhagavad Gītā* (6.13-14)

13. *samaṃ kāya-śiro-grīvaṃ dhārayann acalaṃ sthitaḥ*
saṃprekṣya nāsikāgraṃ svaṃ diśaś cānavalokayan

14. *praśāntātmā vigata-bhīr brahmacāri-vrate sthitaḥ*
manaḥ saṃyamya mac-citto yukta āsīta mat-paraḥ

13. Holding his body, head, and neck in a straight line, steady and without moving, he should concentrate on the point of his nose whilst not looking in any direction.

14. With his whole being in a state of tranquillity, free of fear, steady in his vow of celibacy, controlling his mind, with his thoughts concentrated on me, the practitioner must sit there, dedicating himself to me.

Although the *Bhagavad Gita* makes little mention of the physical yoga practices, which are much more common today, in this verse Krishna describes a steady posture for yoga meditation, which is not entirely different from the lotus position assumed by modern practitioners. The focus of concentration should lie at the top of the nose, between one's eyebrows; this could be taken as a reference to the *ajna chakra*, which is often called the third eye chakra. Through a state of tranquillity, free from all fears, and offering oneself wholly to Krishna (here identified as the *atman*), the practice of meditation becomes a process of self-purification, and leads to a state of infinite inner peace in which the mind becomes absorbed in the *atman*. It is at this point that the theoretical knowledge gained from the *Upanishads* becomes realized knowledge, and the *atman* becomes the sole reality.

ENGAGED IN YOGA

69. *The Bhagavad Gītā* (6.18)

18. *yadā viniyataṃ cittam ātmany evāvatiṣṭhate*
nispṛhaḥ sarva-kāmebhyo yukta ity ucyate tadā

18. When the practitioner controls the mind (*citta*), and fixes it on the *ātman* alone, untouched by any desire at all, he is then said to be properly engaged in yoga.

In line with the ideas encountered in Patanjali's *Yoga Sutras*, Krishna defines the state of yoga as a controlled mind directed at the *atman*. He goes on to describe this state as being just like a lamp which does not flicker in the wind. Once achieved, this ultimate position is never lost, steadying the mind and intellect, and allowing one to work without any selfish desire. This ultimate position is one of joyfulness, in which all suffering ends; hence, it represents the state of consciousness we should all aspire to achieve. This may seem to be very different from the ideas on dharma discussed in earlier verses, but it is apparent that one who transcends all desires is best able to live the dharmic life, and to dedicate himself to the wellbeing of the world.

KUNDALINI

70. *Gorakṣa Śataka* (50-51)

50. *prasphurad bhujagākārā padma-tantu-nibhā śubhā*
prabuddhā vahni-yogena vrajaty ūrdhvaṃ suṣumṇayā

51. *udghāṭayet kapātaṃ tu yathā kuñcikayā haṭhāt*
kuṇḍalinyā tathā yogī mokṣa-dvāraṃ prabhedayet

50. Thus aroused, this energy that has the form of a serpent, and is pure like the filament of a lotus, is then awakened by the fire of Yoga, and moves upwards along the Suṣumṇā channel.

51. Just as a person who has the key can open a door through forceful means (*haṭha*), so the *yogin* should break down the door of liberation by means of the Kuṇḍalinī.

The *Goraksha Sataka* is a treatise on the philosophy and practice of yoga, which was written by the sage Gorakshanath at some date between the 10th and 13th centuries AD. It gives details of the indwelling spiritual force called kundalini. This dormant energy is often described as having the form of a coiled serpent resting at the base of the spine. When awakened, this corporeal energy rises up through the chakras (energy points), and has the potential to carry the spiritual practitioner to the highest state of consciousness. The type of Hatha Yoga taught by Gorakshanath is different from the classical yoga of Patañjali, and prescribes forms of practice such as asanas (postures), pranayama (breathing exercises), and meditation to rouse the kundalini. There are, however, many differing methods and schools of thought for this awakening process. In the 1960s, when a disciple of Neem Karoli Baba asked him how one could raise the kundalini, he simply replied, 'Feed people.'

DESTINY VERSUS ENDEAVOUR

71. *The Mahābhārata* (13.6.7)

7. *yathā bījaṃ vinā kṣetram uptaṃ bhavati niṣphalam*
tathā puruṣa-kāreṇa vinā daivaṃ na sidhyati

7. Even though the field is tilled, a seed has to be sown for it to germinate. Similarly, destiny has no effect without human endeavour.

Are the results of our actions due to providence or due to our own endeavour? This is a timeless question, and here the advice of the sage Kripacharya is that both are required in unison for a successful outcome. He goes on to say that nothing good has ever come from idleness, or relying on destiny alone. Only one who engages in action has the potential to support life, and achieve success. By working hard, by doing everything possible to ensure that the field is carefully prepared and the seeds of success are sown, we create the best possible circumstances to align with destiny. We cannot entirely defy the force of destiny, but success will only come to those who make the appropriate endeavour.

FOLLOWING THE SANATANA DHARMA

72. *The Mahābhārata* (18.5.49-50)

49. *ūrdhva-bāhur viraumy eṣa na kaścic chṛnoti me*
dharmād arthaś ca kāmaś ca sa kim arthaṃ na sevyate

50. *na jātu kāmān na bhayān na lobhād*
dharmaṃ tyajej jīvitasyāpi hetoḥ
nityo dharmaḥ sukha-duḥkhe tv anitye
jīvo nityo hetur asya tv anityaḥ

49. With arms raised, I cry out, but no one hears me. From dharma come both wealth and pleasure, so what purpose could be served by not adhering to dharma?

50. One should never abandon dharma for the sake of pleasure, out of fear, or because of greed, nor even for the sake of life itself. Dharma is eternal, but joy and misery are not; the living being is eternal, but the cause of his existence here is impermanent.

At the culmination of the *Mahabharata*, sage Vyasa gives his final plea for the benefit of us all. To wake us from our slumber, he cries out to us to realise that it is only from a state of dharmic consciousness that our true purpose in life can be achieved. In this verse, we are not only taught that dharma should prevail, but that if it does the other goals of life, including pleasure and wealth, will also be achieved. If dharma prevails, there will be no enmity, and there will be no fear; there will be virtue, love, and compassion for all. It is this type of world which would also provide a better platform for economic prosperity, and a better quality of life for all. Not only these verses, but throughout this entire work, what we are offering is a plea for Sanatana Dharma to prevail. It is an attempt to plant and nurture the seed of dharmic consciousness in the world so that all living beings may benefit.